AF442914

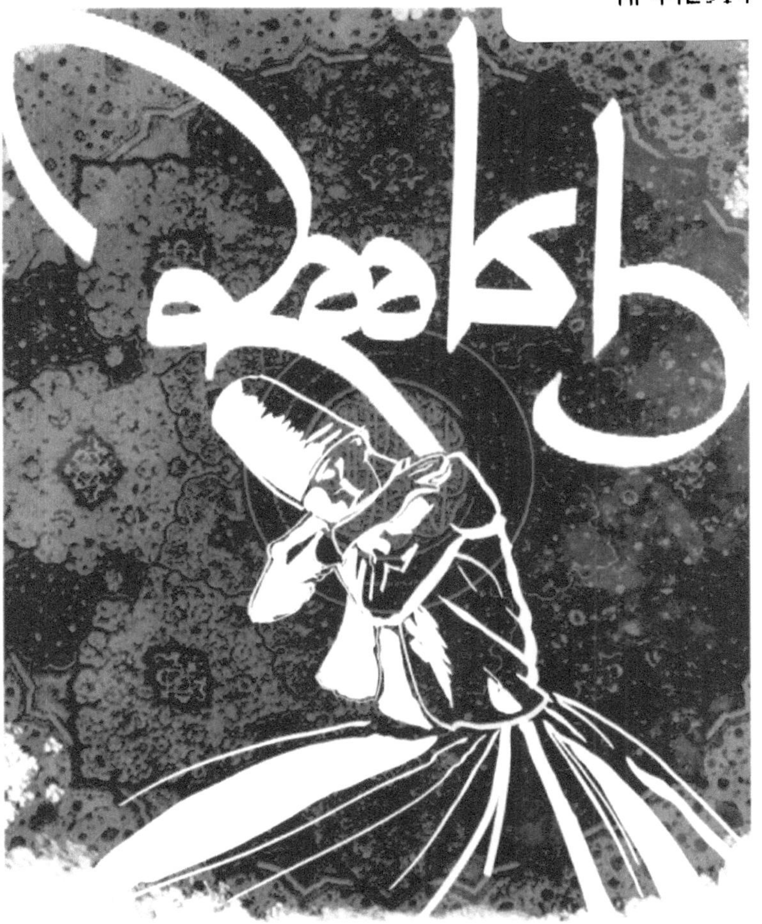

Daakh

illustrated by Aniruddha Chakraborty

sohom paul

Copyright © Sohom Paul 2023
All Rights Reserved.

ISBN 979-8-88883-668-2

This book has been published with all efforts taken to make the material error-free after the consent of the author. However, the author and the publisher do not assume and hereby disclaim any liability to any party for any loss, damage, or disruption caused by errors or omissions, whether such errors or omissions result from negligence, accident, or any other cause.

While every effort has been made to avoid any mistake or omission, this publication is being sold on the condition and understanding that neither the author nor the publishers or printers would be liable in any manner to any person by reason of any mistake or omission in this publication or for any action taken or omitted to be taken or advice rendered or accepted on the basis of this work. For any defect in printing or binding the publishers will be liable only to replace the defective copy by another copy of this work then available.

For

Ms. Arunima Paul,
Mr. Clive Andrews, and
Mr. Lincoln Druart.

Teachers, storytellers, and inspirations.

Contents

Ishq: There is no one word, for sometimes One is many.

Aqeedat: Trusting loyalty

Ibaadat: Worship

Junoon: Madness

Maut: Death

Preface

There are words I don't know ever having existed. I wouldn't, couldn't, can't, won't, don't, mustn't know what they look like, sound like, and feel like.

This is not a good place to be in, let alone for someone who cares about words and what they make someone feel. I don't have a word for how that knowledge makes me feel. What I have instead is the fleeting idea of walking down one of many corridors in a house that I don't know exists, past doors I couldn't have known were there. I can't know what's behind any of those doors, and most likely won't find out what's behind the doors that I don't see.

Sometimes, in this idea of things that I don't know about, I know some doors I mustn't open. Corners I mustn't turn. Things I can't hear and see.

Things that can feel what it's like to have me wordlessly grow smaller and smaller as I walk through them with the Sun setting past the rustling trees.

Words have magic.

But we can't wait for miracles.

We have other places to be in.

Places we know exist. Places we may not have hoped to find ourselves in, but care about.

Sometimes a place is a person. Sometimes a person is an idea. Sometimes ideas are words.

This place, of black and white, is a place that I didn't know would come to exist. I have, however, walked its corridors and halls for years. Found myself pushing open a door to a room, finding an old chair caked with dust and fingerprints I couldn't remember placing upon it, dragging it into the sliver of sunlight, and starting a conversation.

I can't tell with whom though. We spoke of things. Things became ideas became people became places became a book of poetry.

Sometimes, they become stories you didn't expect, that don't look, sound, nor feel so much like stories, much like this:

> *Quite lost, really, some would even say distracted and distraught; was the Man.*
>
> *Walking down the same old paved roads that he knew so well that he could point out misplaced pebbles and uprooted tiles with acute precision, he was lost.*
>
> *He turned left then, and walked down a road no one had yet come upon.*
>
> *Walking straight, he stumbled twice or thrice on the ruddy path.*
>
> *His shoes hurt, so he took them off.*
>
> *He turned and gazed into a direction that did not exist, and with a smile to his lips, jumped across the pavement walls onto the garden path.*

In the garden, the Man discovered a miniature rainbow of sorts, shimmering in the droplets of the sprinklers.

He straggled closer and leaned in.

Perhaps too close, for he

Toppled in head first, and disappeared in the colored haze.

(In slow motion, you can imagine a man fading in a rainbow the size of your foot):

First the head, then the torso, then the arms followed by hands;

Fingers waving and then clenching.

Flailing legs moist with dew and clumps of mud.

(Imagine this with a blurry camera effect with neutral colour tones merging to sepia as the toes vanish and so does the Man.)

A depression on the grass shows where he'd been standing just a moment ago.

That too fades, the blades of grass rising proudly again and a sweet fragrance of bleeding grass Filling the air around the garden,

Mild breeze nursing the wounded strings of grass to life.

And they lived happily ever after.

This is a book about happily ever afters, and what comes before and after.

This is a book about love. And what comes before and after.

This you must know, and expect.

I'm afraid I have forgotten about, and realise now that I should have also had an -

…Introduction

If you've found yourself by pure happenstance on this very page, with a voice quietly asking:

What is this book and why is this called Raakh?

I promise you, you're not alone, and therefore, I'm not alone too. I call this book Raakh because-

well, no, more important than the name, is what this book is:

This is a book of Love, the way it is spoken of by Sufi saints and poets.

This is a book of poems, set in seven different chapters.

These are poems I wrote over the years, but you'll see more of that soon, anyway, poems about love, mostly. They're divided into the seven chapters, each dealing with the seven stages of Sufi love: *Attraction, Infatuation, Love (kind of, but not entirely just that), Loyalty, Worship, Madness*, and *Death*. You could choose to read them in any order you'd like, and to be perfectly honest, I wrote them in any order I found them in.

I didn't know I was writing this book when I was writing the poems, and I couldn't have known how they'd come together. And yet, these things that I made up have come together, and therefore, I can pretend that I knew what I was doing all along, which is my little secret that I've now committed to print.

Long before I knew this book would be, I knew what I would call it. I imagine that's what people do with their children, or their dreams. Names, by the virtue of being words, have magic, and saying them sometimes makes them feel real. Places have magic, and calling them by a name sometimes makes them feel real, or not.

There is an overarching theme, but I'll not spoil it for you. I will, however, tell you about some of the poems here, and if you're the kind of person who reads introductions, you'll know something more about them, from what I know of them.

Gunfire Galaxy

I read somewhere that outer space smells like gunfire and barbecue. I liked that idea, even if it wasn't true. On the eve of a new year, as I sat looking at the fireworks from the rooftop of an old restaurant in some alley of Old Delhi, I wrote this one. It was borne out of a black and white photograph my friend and sister Jhilam had clicked of me tottering down the stairs, and it reminded me of falling into a familiar place. I knew this place, just not what I'd call it. It had a name, and it perhaps sounded like Love.

Cinamon

I wrote this in Rishikesh, for someone I hadn't met. It's named after Cinamon Hadley, the Girl Who Was Death, who was a Goth ballerina Goddess from Salt Lake, Utah. She was a beacon of Love, and Life. She died on 6th January 2018.

Tainted Glasses

One of my parents got me a kaleidoscope when I was a child. I was fascinated, then bored, then terrified of it. I always had a problem with shapes I didn't understand then, which perhaps extended to my fear of strangers too. As I grew, these shapes changed, and the way they came together and fell apart changed. Socrates said something about them at some point in history. Anyway, this is about coming crashing together with rose-tinted glasses on while an unseen hand moves the pieces around.

Down

I wrote this on someone. Like, on the surface of someone. We were drunk, and sinking in a place we were familiar with. This one is about ancient love, and how when it is that way, things tend to grow on your surface too.

Cloudburst Correspondence

This is about familiar scents and things that have a tendency of finding their ways to your pillow. I wrote this while I was loveless, in the middle of a fling, as a goodbye note I never intended to send.

Let's Not Call It

Love is sometimes a thing you can't call by name. Sometimes, you don't intend to find love, because that kind of act needs brevity and faith to come out of the place you've made home. I've called not-Love a lot of things. One of those things was

Tonic, something we made up as a term for what we were. This one actually happens to be a favourite of mine.

The House on Apocalypse Avenue

There is the kind of love that you hope outlasts an apocalypse. This poem was born out of an Indie song I heard, an evening at my favourite bistro, and the prospect of two people who had been in love before finding love again in each other. So what if there was an apocalypse coming someday? You still have your books and coffee, and those little things you go out and bring back home. It's comfortable. It's Love. It's going to stay past the apocalypse, past the drowned sailors who were caught in the end times and settled at the bottom of the ocean.

Salt and Stardust

Salt and Stardust was originally titled "Typw of Lvoe". It was a poem made of typos, for someone who made a lot of typos. I can tell you about the astronaut here. He used to be someone else, some people else. One of those people was a dervish. He grew up learning, loving, searching, and finding answers. Sometimes though, by the time you've found answers, you tend to forget the questions. He is one of them, and now he searches for questions. He remembers that there was someone who'd ask him questions, not necessarily whether it was someone or someone else. He remembers some things, and all of them, through Love.

He's also on the cover, and in many lifetimes, in the pages of this book.

My dog DID help me write this. But wait, I haven't told you about Goldie. Raakh wouldn't be without her. She came into my life, like a story, when you'd least expect it.

I don't particularly remember when I started writing poetry, but I'd imagine it was long before I met my dog. Her name is Goldie, and having known that, you now know that she is real. She goes by other names, and I once had another name for her in mind, I forget what though now.

I don't imagine she remembers too, sometimes she doesn't remember any of her names, or doesn't let me believe she does. In those moments, she's staring out through her brown eyes at a perfectly plain corner of the wall, or at the gentle rustling of the trees, or sinking her teeth into my slippers with the brevity reserved for wolves and children.

It was in June 2013 that I first put any poem out there in the world, where I imagine it is still lost, on a blog. I've slipped in and out of poetry since then. In 2013 I was heartbroken by something that I can't now remember, but I did write then about deserts, about death and dust and divinity, and oceans.

I remember this particular day however, because that's the first time I'd feared I'd lose Goldie. She'd gone off the leash, barking, chasing a stray cat around the corner of the house, leaping past a nasty shrub, headfirst into a wall, and having sneezed her bamboozlement off (because that's what dogs do, they're bamboozled; the internet said so) found her prey perched gingerly atop the wall.

The cat looked gingerly down upon Goldie, who in turn looked back at me, as if to say,

"Are you seeing this?!"

I was.

She leaped at the cat, who was just out of reach. This cat had clearly seen enough cartoons, and thus knew what she was doing.

"FSCHHHHHSSSSHHH!" she said, and supported her claim by baring her teeth.

She had a point, and Goldie concurred.

"Boof", murmured Goldie, and came back to me.

I sighed in relief.

For a fleeting moment, I was happy.

However, I remember the weight of sadness and abandon through 2013 to 2016. I cannot name the reasons for this long sadness, but perhaps that's for the better, for they appear less real for having become nameless. Most of the poems back then were very, very sad, even as I read and re-read them. The memories of what I was doing when I wrote them faded, but the poems remained, somewhere out there and lost to the world.

I changed cities in 2016.

I changed love too. And with that, came the poems of love.

Love, having known it beforehand, felt different, each more different than the last. Goldie wasn't with me then, for she was with my mother, and I missed her, wondering if she still chased cats. I found new reasons for sadness. I found a way to get Goldie back with me in 2017.

She came with my mother, and we lived in this old house somewhere near a forest.

In 2019, I had a heartbreak again, and lost all my poems in a fire. Two separate incidents, I promise you. I wrote then about ghosts, and fire, and dust and ashes, and love.

In 2020, I promised myself to publish, in an act of brevity against the constant cycle of losing and forgetting. To no small part, this was also because I knew what I wanted to do.

In 2008, I had a diary that I trusted with every secret. In it, I wrote about how I felt when the diary was read by someone who wasn't me, and in it I wrote:

"I know what I want to be. I want to be an author."

It was neatly written in dark blue ink, underscored with a signature I've forgotten how to make.

In 2020, I was not an author yet, and the world was shut down, with me in it.

What I was, was a person with dreams, and love, and the constant trail of ashes and dust of things. Things have names, for we must hope for magic.

Raakh was the name of these things put together, for it was a reminder that things can sometimes go away, be destroyed, but have a way of finding their way back. Things, poems, in particular, have a way of finding their places.

I changed my house in 2021.

On one of our late night walks, Goldie and I chanced upon the local cat that diligently visited every house that had a milk basket, and had her way with the baskets. Goldie ran off the leash again (yes, I need to buy a new leash and a set of fingers. Do you have any reliable retailers?) and gave chase. She turned a corner too fast, and I lost her. I yelled her name, and heard nothing back.

In 2021, I lost Goldie again.

She found her way back to me almost half an hour later, covered in leaves and branches, an abandoned slipper between her jaws. I never saw the cat again.

For all I know, Goldie may or may not have concurred with the cat. She didn't remember she was Goldie then, so I'll never know.

On the night that I'm writing this introduction, I feared she'd do just that, for I have now taken to walking my dog without a leash in the middle of the night when there is nobody around. I turned the old corner I lost Goldie a year ago, with her sniffing shrubs along the way, looking for cats and cat food.

She's taken up the habit of eating cat food that people leave strewn around for the local cat

And there, around the corner, was the cat.

I feared the worst.

My dog ate the little nibbles of cat food, for she did not see the packet they came in, and can't tell that it isn't meant for her. She calmly turned the corner, and kept sniffing the bushes while the cat sat tense and frozen.

My dog, I've learnt tonight, remembers what cat food smells like, but maybe not cats.

But then, sometimes, she doesn't even remember her name. Especially when there are other things to remember and think of.

Revenant

Roshni has an animosity towards wild mushrooms, and unbound wonder and love for flowers. This one is about her, and finding a new life in Love.

Not A Day Goes By

I watched Only Lovers Left Alive. In it, Tilda Swinton and Tom Hiddleston are ancient vampires in love. In it, they are destined to come crashing together and falling continents apart, over and over. This poem is about that, and the idea of holding on to every last bit of Love left in us.

Oh, also, some of this is tied back into Troll Witch 2.

Muntazir

I don't remember why I wrote this, but this was the first time I wrote in Urdu. I felt it important to tell you that.

The astronaut whose life and memories we're walking through remembers the language, and sometimes, you'd find him remembering things in it.

Years

Another of my favourites, this is about a man I will meet someday. This man is in love with an ancient, lingering presence, and we meet him on the day of their wedding. He made the leap some of us didn't. But then again, that's the only way he knows how to do it.

He also makes appearances in other poems, if you're looking.

This too is not a Haiku

It really isn't.

Hundred Weeks

I wrote this poem for a spider that's cheating on their overbearing partner in a relationship that is falling out of love. Spiders do talk like that. Read it as you will.

Troll Witch

You must know, this is about someone who has taken all of their suffering, pain, and depression and chosen to task it upon themselves to self therapise. The Troll Witch is a manifestation of that toxic repression and misplaced self therapising that makes you keep bottling these things up, and perpetuating the constant cycle of self-abuse. I've met her, and she's not as friendly as she'd seem. She comes back at the end of it all in Troll Witch 2.

Sundowner Blues

I wrote this in Kolkata, in the South Park Street Cemetery, on a trip I made with the objective of feeling what it's like to be homeless in my city. It was back in 2016, and I had no friends or relatives I wanted to visit. I ended up staying in an art museum, and walking across the city to places I'd rarely been to. I found this poem after reading one too many gravestones that spoke of Love on that day in the cemetery.

Those are some, but not all of the poems I want to tell you about. And now you know of them.

You know now too, that I have a dog who has a complicated relationship with cats. Domestic ones, and the stray ones, that don't know where to go, that belong everywhere and nowhere all and once. Here's a stray poem like them, for you:

I looked to the horizon,
For your rainbow.
Baby,
I couldn't see past your red.

Dilkashi: Attraction

An invisible power in a body by which it draws anything to itself; the power in nature acting mutually between bodies or ultimate particles, tending to draw them together, or to produce their cohesion or combination, and conversely resisting separation.

Gunfire Galaxy

After all this time,
My spirit smells like
Gunfire and barbecue,
Just like they say outer space
Would smell like.
My stars and worlds have come
Crashing together
And fallen apart
Way too many times.
Somewhere,
Debris across my galaxies
Still want to pull together
Near your Sun.
Elsewhere, I'm sitting looking up
At the night,
Wondering where the stars went
After it rained Fire again.

Starfire Muse

In another life,
I'd be reciting Bukowski
With moon men
Who'd only heard of the Sun
In their myths.
In another life,
I'd look at the Sun
From across the universe floating in
Nothingness,
Waiting for an impossible
Shower of meteors, watching a
Thousand Suns, living and dying,
Maybe.
In which of them, would our stars
Not have crossed? In which,
Wouldn't I be on the other side of
The Moon of us?
I'd have known, in another life.

Pyrotechnics

I've met Them who can give men
Butterflies in their stomachs.
And then, there's you…
You.
Oh you, set fire to a man's heart
And the butterflies fly in flocks,
Following in your footsteps.

Swelling

You're that lashing rainfall on a dying summer noon,
That reminds me
There exist fields streaked by lightning
In this realm of fading gold.
That reminds me,
When the days are kind,
Rains like you come visit the grey too.

Cinamon

Darkness is death ignorant,
So careless in your eyes.
October rains,
Find their way there too.

اِقرار (Iqrar)

Jugnu girvi rakh ke
Suraj batorenge kisi shaam,
Aur raakh ke bistar pe
Patte bichha kar soyenge.
Tum milo toh sahi.

Wytch

There hasn't been a winter in years,
That comes as close to shaking my senses,
Reaching the very life gripping my bones;
That can compare to what the mere thoughts of you
Could be capable of.
There hasn't been a winter like you,
That takes me away from me as you do.
If I were any wiser,
I'd pray for religion.

Tainted Glasses

From before Time was real, we were

Always.

Fractal realities shifting in our kaleidoscope.

Here we are Now,

Crashing into each other.

I just don't remember

When we put red glass into our lenses.

Luna

She twitches her nose
And sets aside strands of hair from her face,
As she looks up at the Moon.
The Moon looks right back,
And dreams of Home.

Drifting

The stray scent from the deep of your neck,

On a grey morning with a dash of blue

On a pavement full of strangers

Makes me feel

What a spaceman does,

When there's that snag in the void of outer space.

Shit.

Baby, I'm drifting.

Uns: Infatuation

n. an intense but short-lived passion or admiration for someone or something.

Down

The ancient shores of me
Crumble to the deep of you.
Hermit crabs, and hungry oysters
Make of us what they will.
We're full of each other;
In drowned earth, makeshift homes, hungry mouths,
With pearls of us,
Settled there,
In the dark of us.

Gasp

Won't it be so wild,

If the word put it's mouth on you,

And you didn't say anything back, ever?

How crazy would it be,

If I could climb to the clouds,

Live there like vapours do,

So every time it rains, and the earth has that scent we love,

I don't come running to you with poetry instead?

Imagine if I were rain, coming down in a million drops

Soaking the earth and lingering in petrichor.

Imagine, breathing like we used to,

Then letting go of all that was ever in our lungs and going on
    living,

Forgetting we didn't remember to survive.

Downpours

You really should have called
Before the monsoons came this year.
I was playing with fire when the first drops fell,
And I was left between
Plunging in the river,
Or running for cover
Before my flame went out.

Explorer

She walks barefoot,

Nervous and secretly hopeful;

For she's only started to discover what the world is about.

You can see whole galaxies swing into life in her eyes;

The wonder of a Universe within her smile.

She's the sort you'd sit with, coffee mug in hand,

On a dusty evening,

Watching the stars come up.

She's the sort you'd hold your breath for,

Intoxicated and incinerated,

A speck in her Sun, burning twice as hot.

She's the sort that'd make you wish

You were her Home.

She's the sort, that before you realise

Is both Home and the World to you.

Well, she…

She's just started to discover

What the world is about.

Let's Not Call It

Love…
Is a downpour of colours
In a black and white world,
That's got rows and rows of houses,
With black and white porches.
The rain falls, seeping into the ground
After a while:
Like the beginning of something that
Doesn't turn out to have meaning,
Or the end of something,
Of which the meaning is forgotten.
So let's not call it

Love

Or say

Love

Or think of it.
Because…
After a certain point in time,
We're all houses in a world
That can't grasp colours.
We're all houses that have either been
Lived in

Some, never occupied:
Doors and walls left untouched;
Some, with very persistent tenants,
Still living in the attic or basements.
You can complain: sometimes the walls
Shake,
The floorboards creak,
And the waterworks aren't really reliable.
Sometimes, the way the coffee
Boils in the kitchen
And fills the house with an aroma that
Cannot be forgotten, reminds you of
Things,
That crush like coffee beans inside of you:
Ground fresh each day,
Or maybe each week.
Sometimes, the coffee just lies in the corner
For ages before anyone
Picks it up again.
It's just safe to not call it

Love

Because

Love

Becomes the reason showers and taps
Leak after they've been running too long,
And bedroom walls smell
A particular way
That makes going to sleep
Difficult
Is the reason they hate
Children running around in an
Antique shop: your shields, your perfect
Porcelain dishes, your fine
Glass hearts tremble
And fall
Around their unplanned, imperfect touch.
And as they fall
In a million shining, clamouring pieces,
You learn to count:
This you needed.
That: maybe not.
Those: gone forever.
Till you close the door behind…

Love.

…Take a deep breath.
Start to mop. And make a new list
All over:
This you'll need.
That goes somewhere in the back.

Those…
It's probably a good idea
To put up a bell at the door;
Or maybe a chain.
So, you know,
When someone comes along
You can hold the door open:
Ever so slightly, and with a nose poking
Out of the gap
Ask who it is this time.
"Oh, it's you, what is it?"
"No, now is not a good time."
"Sure, you can come in for a while!"
"Oh, it's You…"
You're almost hesitating to look outside
And hold the door wide open.
It's half disbelief, half memories,
In which you realise:
All the rain and running water
That'd slipped between your toes and past your being,
Has started to seep into the trees
And blades of grass.
It sounds crazy, it sounds stupid,
To see how the puddles in the bath
Take the colour of the floorboard
Between your toes, and make

Little whirlpools as they
Go down the drain.
It's all a cycle.
It all comes back.
And you remember..
You remember, what you'd taught yourself
To count:
This was important.
That wasn't.
Those weren't here anymore.
And

                                                            Love

Reminds you, why you'd learnt to count
And put up the chain in the first place.
Love
Writes you letters, in crayons with
Words that remind you to smile
In a very particular way.
So let's not call it
Love
Because it's always followed
By thunder and lightning,
Rain, beating down and running in gullies.
And the unmistakable moist smell of
Earth.

We'll think up another name:

Give it another meaning,

With our lungs full of petrichor,

Over a hot cup of black coffee…

خشک (Khaak)

Alfaaz raakh ho gaye,
Rooh ki qaagzi naav par,
Ummeed mein ke,
Kabhi toh Jhelum beh jaaye.

Lungs Full

My girl, oh she's so fine!
I met her in the white sea,
Sinking past my last wish,
Holding on my horses,
Flaring all my senses, and I!
I see her from time to time,
Sinking in the darkness,
Drowning out the pauses,
Gasping like a madman.
I'm saying:
"If this is it, if this is all,
If this is the end of ends in the cold bed of all ends,
You must know,
That this little bit;
This little life, this little piece of the worlds that we
Never let go of, this, my love,
Is my favourite of all.
"And if we must go,
We'll go like we were the last of the birds flying home.
"If we must love, we'll love like
The droplets of water in snow.
And if we must die, know that your love

Is all that I know.

"If we must die, know that your love is all.

And I know, I know I'll meet you again…

"Your lungs full of fire and my mouth

Full of smoke.

In a sea full of us,

And warm dreams of snow."

So, Girl!

Won't you be so kind!

We'll meet past the heartbreaks,

And trees of shattered spines.

Oh, when they mourn us they'll mourn us with the Moon and
the stars.

I hope when they mourn us,

We'll look at the Moon

And the stars.

Stable Ends

Me from a few years ago,

Would have promised you storms

That would raise waves in your ocean.

Me from a few years since then,

Wants to be nothing less than the night after

The storms have come and gone.

My stars want to melt and fall into your ocean,

Your's alone, and memorise the waves,

Wild as they come and go;

To become the shimmer that cools into the sunrise

That's borne to dive back into your depths

Every evening.

The beating hooves of nomads,

The cymbals and strings of gypsies,

Isn't my music any more.

I've grown older.

Colder.

The firewood crackling in our corner of the world,

Where the rooms all smell of us, is home.

You're home.

Oh, honey,

We're Home.

خمار (Khumaar)

Kuchh toh cheez hai qayamat,
Kuchh toh hai tabahi.
Aur ek tum ho,
Jiske liye saans khatm ho jaye,
Par rago se nasha na chhute.

Cloudburst Correspondence

Your rainfalls are tucked
Under my pillow.
I've left there our letters.
I guess by now, the addresses have washed out.
Someday, when I change cities,
I'll forget where they came from and
Where they were going.
Someone else would put their heads there,
And listen to distant thunder.

Alchemy

I've mixed too much of You
In too little of me.
So much, that the littlest moments are
Saturated
With what they should be like,
Were You here.
Only if You were here.

Ishq: There is no one word, for sometimes One is many.

The act of being pierced by love and finding romance verging on the divine.

The House on Apocalypse Avenue

On the day the world was dying,

You said,

"Let's build a home.

We'll buy rice lights and lanterns.

We'll string them on the ceiling,

We'll get our bags,

Make pillows out of them, and sleep on the floor, tucked in close.

On the day the earth started to tilt,

I said,

"I know someone who sells stolen

Lights, and tangerine love. We can sell our magazines and old albums

And maybe,

We can get that civet coffee

We've always wanted."

So that was that. On the day the polar bears joined the

Cabaret act, we made our home with our precious album covers and breeze-blocks.

On our walls and windows we strung dreamcatchers and wind chimes

And in the living room, two pre-owned hearts

Home smelled of coffee, and your morning breath, of all things
    i'd wake up for, and

Place on my lips without provocation.

On the day the horizon let go,

We watched the ships sail into forever sunsets and storms of
    peace.

You said,

"You're like a book that I wish I knew didn't have pages with
    scribbles and

Folds, baby.

I hate it when people hold a book open too wide licking their
    fingertips as they

Turn the pages.

Placing bookmarks between chapters, and forget they were
    kept

There."

On the day the birds didn't come back for winter,

I held you tight in my arms to stop myself from drowning in
    my sleep.

I said…

I don't remember what I said.

I remember waking ue

My right arm sore

From having you sleep on it, holding you before my fingers lost
    meaning.

I remember, your annoyed breath and beating heart, from my
    lips chasing my love

Across your face to the tip of your nose till it plunged into your
    mouth and was your's.
On the day the sailors drowned in the ocean while bears danced
    on a tilted horizon,
We held each other in bed, fingers laced between fingers,
    waking up and pressing our faces
So close together that our blemishes matched and melted
Between us.
We savoured our breath, our secret treat, crème brûlée sweet.
We found home, with our pre-owned hearts
That smelled of fresh coffee,
And our old books.

Hungry Seconds

We dream.

Our tongues salty,

Eyes full of pearls.

Humming poetry into the night sky,

Rationing time we spend resting our heads

On each other's shoulders.

Fists clenching and melting,

Crushing fingers laced between each other.

Burning cigarettes away

Between shared breaths.

Our failed experiment with cake making

Lingers in the air,

Vanilla sweet,

Finding perfection in our lungs

From the taste of our being,

I could starve with you, my sweet,

And come back, asking for more…

Let's Just Call It

Love…
Is where all ends go to die
Under a sky of dying forevers and honey drenched clouds.
On the day after the world was meant to end
And the last of the ships set sail.

Love,
Is the last letter ever to the Bohemia,
Locked and turning yellow in a box in a city of dementia,
Where we go to bed to blink the sleep out of our eyes,
Remembering every name that meant something, anything,
Anything till the world started calling us what
They'd call a stranger,
Only for us to turn and look telling them
This is the last ever.

Love,
Between our breath as we cut ourselves till we flow like rivers
into seas into oceans
Till the world drowns and the salt on our cheeks taste like
home.

Love

Is daddy issues upon daddy issues upon daddy issues upon
    mommy issues upon daddy issues,

And only one cuddle away from putting it all and our bones
    together away from finding the one issue.

Love,

Is running down the gullies and foxgloves in bloom,

Splish splash whooshing through puddles once the rains came
    and went,

Drawing maps of goosebumps hand in hand in faith in prayers
    in gasps in our breaths

In hot pursuit,

Till we find Home.

So let's just call it

Love.

And say Love.

Because Love…

Is why we steal kisses under cedar shingled roofs;

Sweet, warm, pure between passing heartbeats trickling

Honey,

How we breathe and sigh,

Under grey blankets and hallucinate photos in Polaroid,

So when they find us when we're gone,

They'll still get the colour of the wool right,
And dream of how it could have been under it
And never get it quite right, not how it is.

So we'll call it Love,

Because in naming Love
We name Us, and all that we call Our's.

Because

Love
Is all dressed up and everywhere to go
So we make a Korean date night at home with
Cheese entangled forks and post rock
Over our heartbeats

Because, damn it, Love

Becomes the reason we hold on
To our favourite blankets and bedsheets and flowers
That remind us what it feels like, what it smelt like, what it
    looks like
And we spend nights sleepless
Drenched in the sweat of faith

With the flood at our doorsteps.
Remembering our names but not just right until

Love

Smears
Honey on our lips, smoke in our lungs,
And we quote poetry and pray to what
Icarus prayed to, wax blazing trails on his back,
Feathers fleeting like prayers in a tongue that's forgetting letters
Just out of reach.
Death glowering like a furnace in our breath,
We light candles,
So we can remember:
Love,

In our being.

Love,

In our faith.
Love,

In saved up coins and trinkets and flowers pressed between the
    pages of our favourite books;
In places uncountable and in the promised land of goosebumps.

Love,

In evenings of rain under a sky painted in honey and waxen
    screams of

Love.

Whisper with me,

"Forever",

"Your's",

"We're home",

"I've got you".

"Don't go".

"I love you, please".

Because baby,

When it's cold out, it's warm between our fingers.

Warm here. Warm with you.

Warm in our forevers.

Oh, Love,

Scatters like the last pomegranate in our midnight raids

In the cold light of the fridge:

Red pearls of our forevers

Gathered in a mad scramble and consumed,

Bleeding through our lips

As it rains again tonight.

We dance, spinning in circles

To our favourite songs,

Our favourite steps,

Our   god-I-could-never-let-people-see-this-don't-you-dare-
    record-this-I-will-

Kill-you-if-you-do!

And laugh.

And laugh.

In a world,

That knows not Love,

The way Icarus did,

The way we do,

Because Love,

Love,

Is not just fucking it's making love

With the lights on

Till we know we both find home.

Love,

Is what we are,

When the skies painted in meteors and a thousand Suns

Come crashing down upon our Home

And the oceans sizzle and boil.

Baby,

Love
Will remember Us.
When they find us when it's all over,
Forever
In black and white.

Salt and Stardust

Somewhere out there
There's an astronaut in outer space, drifting among the Stars
Looking down at the radiant Earth, and remembering
Home.
There's probably a storm circling
Right above where his home is,
Where things will never be as bright in real life
As they are in his memories, his dreams.
He dreams.
There,
It's always just about to be sundown,
With the dust settling on the horizon:
The children coming home,
The dogs racing and jumping at their little footsteps.
He probably dreams of his little goldfish in a round fish bowl
That he chose and paid for,
On a bright summer day at the local pet store back home,
Tippy-tapping giddily back with the dogs playing at his heels
Before everything changed.
Where he is now, it's always night,
And there's always stars out.

The Sun doesn't cast a rainbow anymore.

The Moon…

Doesn't matter,

Where he's going.

From down here, you won't see him,

And his dreams are as far from you

As the Stars and Moon are to him.

But still, they're His, and he's Their's.

It's that type of Love, that makes things dark and deep

Come closer.

Makes the ocean

Tremble

And edge closer to the shore when the Moon is full so the
    tourists gather

With cameras, plimsolls, rugs and children,

With a bunch of stuff ready to be moved or abandoned

At the slightest hint of a flash flood

Or a rogue wave.

It's the type of Love that drowns.

The one that takes you underneath if you're not careful,

Twisting you around and the

AIR

COMES

RUSHING

FORTH

From your lungs to the edge of your lips,

Sailing up to the surface in bubbles that mean the world to you,

And nothing to the loud brimming force of grey

That drags Death from the shore, grain after grain after broken
pieces of shell after grain

Into the waves that consume You.

It's Love.

I feel it on nights like these,

Drowning drifting gulping discovering each drop of Your
oceans.

In You, I let my breath go.

And when the words spill from my lips,

You…

You speak in waves, enough and too far in between to send
tremors

In the world of a Lover.

Wide eyed, tide after tide brined with curiosity, you ask to each

"I love you",

"Are you sure? How much?"

A child could stretch her arms

as wide as they can go,

And it'd be that much.

Centuries ago, civilisations would sink

And the First Men would venture out of their dark caves,

Seeking someone like you, remembering

Something like You

Before they knew You,

And it'd be that much.

                                 A T-Rex that's never been

able to hug

                                 His mother could do his

best to hold

                                 The last of the asteroids,

And it'd be that much.

The wolves could run wild in the open mountain,

Howling at the Moon for millennia

While the sirens blared in the falling cities under the hooves of
    antelopes

That never tire,

                      And it'd be that much.

I'd run out of examples, in this lifetime,

And each other, all the while drowning deeper in Your ocean,

Uttering the words,

                      And it'd be that much.

You're the Dream of Stars and Moons that leaves trails of
    stardust in its wake.

I could make a path across the galaxies paved in Your stardust,

                      And it'd be that much.

You're the type of love, baby,

That makes every ocean and distance fade in comparison as
    words gush forth

Past every breath and I learn to

Pray.

You're all of that,

And the salt from the Ocean that lingers in my veins,

Making its way into my prayers.

You're all of that,

And more than that much.

Favourite Scents

I'd pick the scent of Your skin,
As you turn and brush against Me,
Over the scent of fresh coffee
Every single morning hereafter.

Sundowner Honey

I quit smoking,
Since the day we fell in Love,
And shared our first kiss
Under a tube rose tree in secret.
I get my kicks of nicotine off of your lips,
My addictions and worst impulses laced
In your breath,
Craving every hour for a hit.
And God!
You taste like home,
And I ain't ever complaining
Of being homesick again.
I love how my lungs feel,
Full of You tonight.

Good Morning, Sunshine!

You're the Light that sunrises envy.
All my life,
I've been writing eulogies to each sunrise
That I've missed being with You,
On the back of airplane tickets
And bus tokens
Going Nowhere and Everywhere and Neverwhere,
Too far and too many in between.
I could travel the world so many times over, Baby,
Past so many lives,
Before I make up for all the mornings I've missed
Being with You.

⟶◈◈◈⟵

Aqeedat: Trusting loyalty

n. A state of trusting allegiance and confidence in the Absolute, or the One.

Ghostwriters

My mother talks to my dog,
And my dog writes my lines for me.
She scratches behind her ear.
(My dog, not my mom)
And speaks of the inherent eroticism of the sea.
It's better to drown with your
Lungs full of your own water
Than to have them
Filled with someone else's air
That draws your breath out.
So she says.
She likes long walks
(My dog, not my mom)
It's good for the joints.
She sniffs at roots and tells me,
People are like trees.
They find people who are like
Water and wind.
Herself, she glows in the sunshine.
She likes to smell people's feet and
Steal socks
She places her head on my lap,
(My mom, not my dog)

And tells me how her arm
Was broken
She tells me
It's difficult to walk now,
But when her feet were like
Breeze,
She knew a pathan who was madly
In love with her,
She tells me about how they met
At a mosque,
And that maybe he still prays for
Her, to this day.
On cloudy days, she insists i go
For a walk because we love the
Smell of freshly dampened earth
She doesn't do much around the
House.
She writes my words, and house
Becomes home
Letters and words are
Funny like that.

Ginger

"Cry out your story at every crowded street and crossroads!"
Said the Gingerbread Man.
"Even if you think no one is listening," he said,
Holding out pieces of himself he once called Precious,
To every passerby,
"Somewhere,
It will fit in someday."

Difference

You made a difference.
Then,
Nothing made a difference.

Revenant

The hardest part about young love is it growing old.
And leaving.
I think it died a long time back,
Buried between bones and places where dreams go to,
When dreamers sleep no more.
Seasons kept changing
And so did my body with them,
Gathering dust and earth.
There were occasional flowers and moments of quiet,
And Amens crushed between teeth and cigarettes.
On certain nights,
The flowers bloom in my joints and
I'm crippled in the ecstasy of forgetting what it means.
On certain days, the way it rains makes the earth lay bare and
Send up the Salah the flowers ate,
And we dream a childhood in petrichor,
Flashing back reel-like over
Whirring, clicking breath and heart.
A lot of love isn't remembered in images, but in bones, breath,
And deaths therein.
A whole lot of love isn't held in arms, but in shallow bones,
    dried flowers pressed between pages of books growing old,

And cracked lips that were once whole.

All of love

Becomes a ritual of revisiting and rediscovering, fevered chanting of names and promises.

The safest of love I've gained,

Is in the mercurial madness of you,

And somehow, you've a thing with finding flowers, stopping by, and saying,

"Look! Flower!" and with a pregnant pause

Enough to draw an Amen, you say,

"Can we keep it? I'll put them in resin and preserve them like I used to!

Pretty flower!"

So we collect them, each day.

I rescind my Amens, each day.

I'm finding new worlds with new religions, each day.

In this life, I may make a revenant yet.

⟨⟩⟨⟩⟨⟩

Drowned

The eternities of our yesterdays
Are ashes rolling in the winds of today.
I'd breathe it all in,
But I'm too full of you still
To give up suffocating.

Cats and Dogs

"Miaow!"

"Hurrrph."

Wiser words, darker secrets,

Lovelier sounds were not heard,

Save that night,

Between the cat on the wall and the dog on the porch.

She shone,

Like the Moon in a night full of scars.

"Do you love me?" she asked,

Knowing the answer she'd always heard and

Knowing answers are sometimes forgotten and unseen.

"I love you to your bones."

Said he, on all fours.

You're too far. I cannot tell sometimes.

How much?"

"Uhmm"

He ran.

Past the house that snored.

Past the hedges he'd marked and remembered.

Past the butchers, and past Timbuktu.

Sometimes it was hard to run.

Because the ocean got in the way.

"Faster than my heart beats,"

He huffed.

"I can't swim," she said.

She stretched her tired legs, and flew him a kiss.

And the ocean learnt

What is was

To have

Waves.

He ran another seven hundred and thirty one days,

Till in the city of oil lamps where moths promised undying love in their

Dance in the halls of Flames,

They rested: She on the roof, He on the balcony.

"Why must it always be the Impossible?" sighed She.

"Because we've done everything that's Possible,

And we chose to keep looking."

"After all this time,

You know you're not getting any younger!"

She stuck her tongue out and shook her head with a smile.

That night,

The moths forgot what Fire felt like;

And out of the darkness under the lamps

Flew out fireflies that filled the sky.

He ran again, this time

Till the end of time.

Past towers of men and boxes of post,

Where he'd stop to lick envelopes,

And send her illegible letters

(Because let's be honest, dogs cannot write all that well, but we digress, while he runs)

Each day, until they met in the city where the river ran past the elysiums,

And they rested at their favourite spot by the river

Like they'd always wanted.

"There's a valley of me," he said,

"Just behind the last mountain of what I was,

Near the ocean of what I will be.

The sky is You.

I can taste you when it rains.

You're where I go, to make the horizon home…

Wave after wave, over and over. And over again."

"I hope we're for real, for I can't spin more yarns,

And this, this feels like home,"

She said, in a voice she'd reserved for a few.

She turned her head to him, and in his eyes,

Saw only herself.

In her eyes, the shade of ancient roots,

He saw colours.

"There's something I've always wanted to do with you", he said,

Taking her paws into his,

Stepping towards the river bank.

"I can't swim!" she shook her head and trembled her whiskers.

"I can't drown," he smiled, "and this is true."

"Now tell,

Tell me about your days," said he,

As the river flowed past his flank.

She spoke.

She shone.

She stretched.

She smiled, and looked him in the eyes and they

Untied

Each knot they'd gathered over their lifetimes.

It felt unreal, so much, that when it started to rain,

And the scars fell off the sky and washed away in the river,

No one took notice.

There were them.

There was the sky.

There was the ocean filling to the brim,

Flooding the valley,

With every drop of her.

"Miaow."

"Ruff."

Halcyon Lovebirds

She curls up
In Her favourite corner of the house,
And She makes it Home.

We eat words out of each other's mouths;
Morsels and strings dangling between our lips,
The vapours of Our words tangled with
The vapours of Our breath
Under a pale moonlight that's
All Our's.

Her words are the lost coins in trouser pockets We keep in a pile
At the corner of the room;
My voice laces with the smoke of my cigarettes and when
I pop the little bead of menthol,
My voice is the cold, cold dark of the night.
We're Our favourite flower,
Our favourite songs,
Sizzling like a lump of hot charcoal
Carelessly tossed into a glass of cold, cold whiskey.

We're Smoke.

We're swallowed in Kisses with our Mouths full of Smoke.

We're

Drunk.

We're Melting.

We're Home, and so good at getting lost.

We make Love, dark and fragrant,

And the Lost Coins somewhere in a pile feel shiny in Our
afterglow.

We're Smoke and Mirrors.

And usually hungry after words.

Not a Day Goes By

Not a day goes by
Without me thanking the universe
For Your mouth, and it's sickly heat.
You've been through lovers like seasons, Love.
All of them burning, fading, leaving,
Melting at the taste of your fever pitch warmth.

And yet, there's love in each drop of your saliva
And I must confess,
If the world were to end tomorrow,
I'd want to head into the nothingness drunk on the last drops of

Our precious, precious Kiss.

That way, I'd remember it forever, even as I'm turning into
    Nothing.
I want you to know, if there was one wish I'd die to see come
    true,

It would be Death

With the codeine sweet of you, in my last atoms.

It's terrifying, how one goes about their whole lives without
    knowing
What it's like inside of You.
No, wait, is it more terrifying, to have known,
And go about the rest of their lives without You?

I don't know.
I wouldn't know.
But I do know,
If the world were to end, and we met again,
And You with your evil, evil eyes asked:
"Remember me?"
I'd point here, and Here, and here,
To every last love drunk atom that keeps coming back for you,
That refuses to learn otherwise, and say:
"I do. Here. And here."
I'd say, "I've been trying to pluck my bones out
To hold them in my palms
To remember what it was like to hold something, anything,
    that mattered"

I'd say, "Not a day goes by…"

⸺⟡⸺

Unavoidable, Unforeseen, Indescribable Circumstance

You're what most people would describe as an
Unavoidable circumstance.
There were no two ways about You.
And for me, there were none
As You walked into my life,
Footsteps ablaze.
You burnt some bridges,
And anything that had come before You
Laid in ashes.

منتظر (Muntazir)

Hum hi toh qaatil thehre khud ke,
Ke dhool raakh ki kahaniyo mein
Dafnaaye rakhe wajood,
Aur qalam bhi baat te phire un haathon mein
Jinme ghutan likhi thi.
Panno pe panne sajaaye qitaab rahe
Naqab banaye panne sajaaye baithe rahe.

Sach toh ye hai ki
Alfaaz bas aarsi parsi faarsi se hai,
Adhoore panno pe panne bepanah padhe rahe.
Aap bhi bas…palat te jaiye,
Agar alfaaz kabhi khatm hote dikhe,
Dil kare toh qalam utha lijiye.
Rang dijiye alfazon ko kaale aur safed mein.
Panno ka kya hai, rango ki unhe kaha penchaan.
Haath thak jaye, dil ruk jaye,
Saans bhar aaye, toh ruk jaiye.

Kisi din phir dil kare, qitab uthaiye.

Panno pe panne padhte jaiye,
Kuchh panne aap ke, kuchh panne hamare,

Kuchh panne ajnabi se aur
Kuchh panne bepanah yu hi.

Sookhi syahi ki kahaniyo ki vaado ke intezar mein,
Meri wajood bhi hai bepanah dafnaye.
Us me rang kaale safed ghulte huwe
Sapno jaise fanaa rahe,
Alfaz bhi,
Tinka bhi,
Raakh bhi.

Ibaadat: Worship

n. Unquestionable love, reverence, and commitment with veneration for the One.

Breakneck

Ain't You the dawn
To the morning the apocalypse came?
Baby,
You're the dusk to the night so dark,
That my heart went missing,
And never came back the same.
Fuck,
I could run into the end of times writing poems of You,
At each time of the day,
And meet my end,
Before I ran out of words
For the last of You.

Not a Haiku

I ran into You and fell in Love,

And I wrote.

I fell and ran out of words,

And I wrote.

Shores

There's a rhyme in the pool of your smile
Where poets go to drown.
I dream sleepless,
In the visions of its shadows.

Luminescence

And then,

I wrote poetry, likening Her to the Sun and the Moon

And stars and storms;

Outright comparing Her to Goddesses and Existence.

I've never stopped since.

None of it was enough,

Never, maybe.

Her (no, not that one)

Just beyond the cloud of aeons
It's ancient Greece:
Philosophers are arguing over the depths of Her spirit,
Caves be damned.
It's 2070 AD:
Scientists are beginning to get hints of the very essence of Life
In Her fingerprints.
It's feudal era Japan:
Where fox spirited ninjas are infused with the spirit of passion
    and vigour,
By Her voice.
It's a courtyard in ancient Persia:
Where dervishes dance for hours in a trance,
Of the scent of Her breath and sweat.
It's nothing and anywhere at the End and Beginning:
The loom spins, forever and never,
And just like that,
It's now:
You're crumbling into Her,
Like Atlantis did centuries ago,
Right into the heart of the Ocean, that is
Her.

List of Things the Man Being Shot out of a Cannon Said to His Lover as He Flew Past the Town

The sun soaked evenings
Of Whiskey Boulevard
Have nothing on your breath,
Rising and falling like civilisations so often do.

I'd trade the bittersweet taste of sin
Mixed with cold, cold rum with a sizzling piece of charcoal
    thrown in,
For the touch of your skin, tracing down rivers to the Ocean
    of all life,
That's You.

You, I'd pick over the musings of a Sadhu
From the mind of the universe, and find religion,
Right there between those lips
As we let the smoke from us make the sort of mist that leaves
    one soaked to the bone.
The sweet, sickening screeches of seagulls have never given the
    relief, baby,
To sailors coming home;
The way falling into you gives me,

My sweet death of Nothings.

The galleries of Sultans, my Sweet,

Have nothing on the artwork of trainwrecked Goddesses,

That's You.

⊷◦◦◦⊶

Eight Doors

My fingers touched my ashes,
Touched my dust caked skin from the ride,
As I lowered my head into my
Reflection in the waters of nothing.
I could drink in gulps from the day
I found your body wrapped around
My home, moving gently, breathing,
Under waters still and cool.
I'm going to sink, falling through
Doors the shape of you.
Before the end of us comes, baby,
Can I kiss everything that is you,
That's not
Your skin, hair, and bones?

عبرت (Ibrat)

Qayamat ke arso me rotiya todh rahe hai.
Kya karu ke jab niwale bikhre bhi the
Tab tukde bhi saare tumhare hisse ke the.

New Religion

I'd not worshipped in ages,

Were it not to the altar of love.

There's a comfort to knowing her effigy

Is made of the faith my bones are made of.

Years

I met a blind man in a boat, in the middle of a storming ocean.
Violets in hand, head lowered in prayer,
He said it was his first.

"Storm?" I asked.
"Prayer", he said.

He raised his eyes, grayer than the storm,
Looking at something I didn't recognise.

He said,
"When I was young, I could see.
On an evening when the clouds decided to come down on our
     town
And I had nothing else to do,
I stood by the river near our backyard under a sheet of canvas
     and smelled the
Earth.
I couldn't see the other side of the river.
Nor see what was at an arm's length.
That's when I saw her.

She sat at the edge of the river bank and
Looked over her shoulder.
She looked past the grey water coming from the grey skies and
    the grey mist and
By the time I realised I was uncomfortable,

She said,
"You look different. Pristine. Like you're
Made of another earth now.
You don't remember how the sky looks golden when day makes
    love to night and
Leaves the sky soaked in stars.
You don't. I see you don't."

Her voice, like overflowing gullies ran
Into me and filled me.

"I've been walking the earth,
Making my way to the night that evening would have died in,
And my feet are caked with soil.
My soles are lined with dust
My cheeks are ruddied, and only now I meet you."

Her eyes, like lightning, made their way
Down to my scorched earth soul.

"And today it's raining, washing away my

Soul, bits of me I grew up with.

Washing away my lines and folds I nurtured because you
named them

Precious.

I'll turn to water, then to creeks, then to rivers and then to the
ocean.

It terrifies me, that you shall not walk into me, but stand far
from shore and

Only see the grey.

It terrifies me even more, if you otherwise fall into me, and not
being of

The earth you were, scatter, struggle and regret it as you churn
and

Finally settle into my depths."

The man paused.

He then said,

"Nothing washed me over like that evening.

Not life. Not the death of my cat.

Nor the strings of lovers who promised me an eternity,

And neither the constant

Cloud of grey inside my chest from walking in every rain,

Hoping to feel the same way."

He sat up straight, and fixed his bowtie.

"I'm getting married today,"

Standing up, casting one last look over his left shoulder,
One foot over the edge, he grinned,

"And I can only pray."

Totes

My prayers vaporise in smoke,
Upwards in the sky of you.
I lost my tongue
Somewhere between
Your thighs.

Vinophile Vagabond

I wonder what the seasons are like inside of You.

There's a black umbrella in my consciousness

That I carry in the anticipation of Your summers.

Then, me being all that I am,

I lose it promptly, waiting at the pharmacists';

Or walking lost, in the downpour of You.

You, you, oh…You.

Me being all that I won't be,

I stick my tongue out and taste

Each drop of you.

Drenched in you, homeless and drunk,

See the orchards turn orange

At the touch of Your winters.

Wistful and reminiscent at the same

Time,

Clutching the folds of my coat

That you once noticed and smiled.

I'm the mute madman, that abandons all,

Sitting in the crevices that are soaked in brine and mist,

Damp while the world turns to the crisp

Of the creeping of autumn.

Leaping at the sight of the Moon

In the Dark of Your eyes,
I make Port at the shores of Your lips
(I know, not your favourite wine)
Sickly heat of hell, and deathly sweet,
Honey, I've made home in the cave
In the mountains at Your shores.
When it promises to rain, I make my way down your
Goosebump groves,
Salt upon my tongue,
My bones made of paper,
Lined with poetry of You.
Word after word, breath after breath, over and over,
I'm Yours.

(And You're mine)

بنجاره (Banjara)

Kaisi thi woh sheher,

Dilo se kahi aqsar jaha

Insaano ki aadat thi so jaane ki,

Aur abaadi se zyada

Sapno ke shor huwa karte the

Subaho ko?

Banjaaro ka bhi koi pehchaan toh hoga,

Fitrat thi jinke khabti pairo ki

Un anjaan galiyon me jaane ki

Jaha imaarato pe fitoori aur gulabi

Rang sajte the.

Un galiyon mein ek toh ghar khali hoga

Ke jiski khidkiyo se baarisho ke mausam mein

Chaandni dhal ke aati hai farsh pe

Aur ek muskaan chhu ke khil uthti hai.

Uss sheher ke khawab se dil jaaga nahi hai ab tak.

Mere sheher ke subaho mein

Neend khule toh,

Yaha koi na hai mera.

In Naming You

In naming You,
I forget the names of all else, so the world thinks me mad.

My words find the darkest little crannies to scuttle into
When You're not looking,
And I lose at hide and go seek each day,
Losing a word, a name each day,
Calling out for them with Your name.
I lose, gulping down Your name,
Tongue coated in codeine,
A verseless poet in a spell of late night radio station static.

I drive on till it's dawn,
When I rhyme Your name in mine.
My words gush along your collar bones,
And my throat is pyrene.
I mix You with wine.

What else would I do,
With words that made You home,
Words that are travellers with a sense of direction
Worse than mine?

Junoon: Madness

n. A state of relatively permanent insanity from extreme faith.

Raakh

What of the gypsies, so full of love, they could

Barely eat?

What of the mad ones, the loud ones,

The ones who had their eyes pried open till their

Hearts ran out and their lips

Foamed promises of forever?

What of the blind man, who ran to the horizon with

Naked feet, tossing rocks at the Sun on rainy evenings,

Till the rainbow was the colour

Of his dreams?

What of the drunk ones, who sleep on the sidewalks,

Their speech too slurred to name the ones who didn't write
    back anymore?

What of you, what of me,

Burning in the fires of lust,

Till the smoke filled our city and the earth was left scorched

With the remains of us?

Roller Coaster

Falling in love with you was easy,

Kind of like strapping on the seat belt on a roller coaster.

Then came the whiplash.

The pull at the pit of my stomach.

The tears in my eyes,

And the ringing in my ears.

The urge to hold on for dear life and to never let go.

God!

Falling in love with you…

Was just the beginning.

Phoenix on a Crossroad at the End of the World

I found you,
Minus the navigation system on my phone that I'm so used to.
Minus the constant alarms, that I never wake up without,
Unless it's with you.
And even then, I'm a drooling mess,
Till the first drop of coffee, and the scent of you
Touches my soul.

I'm lost really, and you know what?

I'm good at it!
I'm so good at being lost, that if you were to walk into my life
A second before you did,
I'd be caught in traffic;
A block away from where
Our paths first crossed.

Or, oh, wait,
Did you find me?

Minus the common sense it takes

To avoid all the red flags that line my streets.

Minus the survival instinct that is the last thing

That crosses the mind of a deer that's staring down at a truck

Heading it's way on a highway that used to be near what it called

Home.

Those last moments, I imagine

They're terrifying,

Like the moments were,

Just before we found each other,

Minus the signs that read:

ONE WAY TRAFFIC!

WORK IN PROGRESS!

GO SLOW!

ARE YOU SURE YOU CAN DO THIS?!

Minus the constant voice that tells you, screams at you:

STOP!

WHAT THE FUCK ARE YOU DOING?!?

I wanna tell you, before this off the rails train that's Home

That's Love turns us to roadkill,

You should know,

I love you like flies love each other.

I love you, like seahorses love each other.

Did you know, they mate for life?

Can you imagine that kind of love,

That takes death and wiping off a living being, a whole genetic
code of a living thing,

To fulfill?

That's the kind of love, that's ride or die,

Fuck, marry, kill,

Pheromones roaring,

Forever dancing,

Senses blaring,

Now and forever

Till-the-lights-hit-us-between-the-eyes kind of love,

That you, oh, you…

That's the kind of love you are.

And fuck,

I'd love you to ashes.

Chronophobia

Songs may someday not remind me of you.
More than that day,
I fear the days that may come before.

This too is Not a Haiku

I don't own a boat yet,
But baby,
I'd shipwreck myself at the first sign
Of You.

⸻❧❧❧⸻

Faerie Valentines

She went down the forest lane,
Her hair a mess, her breath aflame.
One last look, above her left shoulder,
And she's gone,
Disappeared in the traces of wispless smoke
From her embers.

"We'll lie down on the grass,
Under the Sun,
Finding horizons that light cannot escape,
Baby. We'll hold hands, and talk about
Madness".

You can hear her still,

"Not the kind of madness that's had
Books written on it. Nah.
We'll talk about the kind that they're still searching a word for."

It's a promise, and she seals with her kisses ephemeral,
Breath laced in smoke,
Smoke laced in love,

Love laced in the heat of the youngest galaxy in the universe,
Brought to life between her lips.

"Look, I've got a spot here!" she points, and I know my way in
    the wilderness.
Her bare feet, they leave universes
In their dust.
Our bare feet, they tingle and grasp
Fleeting sands between them,
As we walk into the ocean where we drown endless and true

"Mine. Thine. Ours."

Those are her words, from her voice,
That like the theremin song on the evening of the apocalypse,
Escape from her lips:
Gateways to places
Where wine-soaked birds fly to their forever sunsets,
And coffee high fireflies find their home where she goes,
Forever waking.
She went down the forest lane,
And wilderness was never the same.

———◦◦◦———

Aghor

The Sadhu collected his slippers from where he'd lose them
     every evening.

He touched fire with his lips, and said,

Every night in his dreams, there is mist.

In it,

Eating hungrily in mouthfuls is something that so devours
     reality

That every morning, a new day brings back cadavers of days
     past.

Of life. Of you. Of me.

Days walk spent in daze into the waiting night where mists roll

And shapes writhe, sharpening fangs and teeth:

Gleaming white in pearly fog.

Nodding heads gargantuan on bodies

Insignificant.

These are my hinterlands. Says he.

These are my dreams, says he.

Here lies my awakening.

Tread soft,

For this terrain breathes with you and knows your ways.

⊶◦❀◦⊷

سیلانی (Sailani)

Gumshuda hai toh wohi sahi
Tumhare galiyon me toh nahi hai.
Lapata hai lekin…
Tumhare zikhr ke siva
Mehroom bhi kaha huwe hai.

Wytch 2

I believe in Magick.

You showed me it,

The first time you turned to cast a casual glance.

And then, years after, certain of the seasons having washed
away the day,

I saw that look in your eyes.

And then,

I knew, just like that,

Gasping in a flash flood of You,

Why lightning reaches down all the way from Heaven

To this world.

Deep Sea Dive

If this'll be the Death of me,

I'll need a drink.

Lungs full of You,

Teeth stained with You,

I'll pretend I can't swim.

Maut: Death

n. Ceasing to be of this life. Maut sometimes comes, like Ishq, in ways you'd not expect.

Hundred Weeks

Baby,
When I. Left through. The window.
While you slept in. Your bed.
Snoring.
Just before the. Last light of dawn.
I. Saw. Knotted to the chair.
In the. Corner of your room.
Our love. Twisted. Coiled. And tied to. My ankle.
It felt like.
The most fragile. Thing. That ever was.
Save your. Breath.
Baby I. Leapt out before you. Woke up.
Clay and dust. On your eyelashes.
I tread. On threads. I must. Glide.
For I. Never wipe my feet.
On my way. Back home.
On your favourite doormat.
Our only. One.
And you know. Dust. So well.
Oh I thin the thread at my ankle.
Each day and. Yet. It stretches.
Theremin resonance.

At my toes.

I promise. I'll be back. Soon as.

The sun goes down. And it's evening.

We will. Watch the dew drops.

In my. Pretty webs that I'd. Leave on. Our skies while we. Sit.
    For tea. I'll sing. To you.

Sit.

I know your favourite chair.

I always come back to it.

When I can't sleep.

Baby.

I get hungry when you sleep.

And dreams don't taste like they used to.

⟨⟩

اضطرار (Iztiraar)

Rang chhoot gaye hai saare aaj film reelo se
Lekin tasveere jo thi, woh ab tak nahi miti.
Wahi kirdaar, wahi harqat, wahi bol chaal
Barkarar hai,
Bas rango ke bina wahi jazbaat, wahi iraade
Aur wahi paigham
Aaj kuchh pheenke se, jhoote se lagte hai
Andhere kamre me.
Rang chhoot rahe hai wajood aur yaddasht ke bhi, aur
Bina geelepan ke bhi sarhade mit rahi hai aaj theater mein
Mujh mein aur gadde ke beech me.
Nalayak ye narmi kaha se aati hai yaad dilane ke
Chamro ke neeche geelepan ke paar kahi kuchh sakht hai jo
Dafnai ke saalo baad tak bhi ratobat nahi haasil kar pati.
Ghafil!
Qafn ke andhere mein aur chite ki ujalo me bhi aakhir
Rang dhundle hi hai.
Aarzi ujaalo aur andhero me jo ungliyan
Khud ki shakal shanakht na kar paye,
Tok aukat kya hai ke hum kahe ke hum khud ke jism me gair
   nahi.

Aukat kya hai ke hum maan le ke
Aaj ghar jaake jab taqiye me dum ghotenge
Tab kam se kam khwaab toh rangeen honge,
Aur khwaabo mein shayad filmon ke yaadein bhi
Taaze rangeen honge.

Troll Witch

There was a Fire
That took to the woods.
Suddenly, there was no place anymore
For things that kept me up at night.
So one day, I made up a Troll Witch.
She'd eat
What I couldn't share with the rest,
Things she'd hold safe in her warm pot belly.
She lived under the arch of a fortress that
Time and humans had razed into ruins.
On days when the Sun is high,
And nights when the Moon is close,
We sit and talk.
She keeps busy,
And we exchange stories.
Most of it is echo.
Most of it comes back,
And the Witch eats another day.
Such is our kindred.
Maybe, the pyres of her arms will someday burn
The Wretch that lives in me.
Maybe, her breath will be the end of my demons.

There's Death in her eyes, baby,

And maybe I'm a ghost that's only lingered on because my soul
won't let go of her.

I'd promise to give my life to her, Love,

And lie looking her right in the eyes,

Had my lungs not been so full of water.

I've forgotten how to die.

I've forgotten how to move on.

After all this while,

I've forgotten how to fall out of love.

I've drowned far too much

To float back up.

12:12

I miss your love bites.
The warmth of wearing you on my skin.
I miss calling you Home,
And learn why
There's such a thing as a homeless problem.

Al-Dimiryath

The Djinn is safe,

Snoring in the slumber of aeons;

Tucked away safely

In a forgotten corner no one visits

Inside a dirty, forgotten lamp somewhere

In an antique store no one comes visiting.

He smiles in his sleep,

A being of powers almost God-like:

Tucked in a dark bed of alloy

Kept warm with rotten oil.

In the fogs of his dreams, wonders the Poet,

What does a being of fables see?

Perhaps…

The Djinn will one day be set free

By a traveller far too curious, a thief far too greedy, a child far
    too naive,

Or a bull far too angry to be indoors;

And then,

Just like he's done time and again, he'll rise

Pouring forth in billowing smoke, vapours of ancient incense,

And stand proud, tall like a giant warrior in a world of ants.

On that day, the lamp will seem like a bad memory half
    forgotten.
The thousand years of stifling and shuffling will be no more.

No.

On that day, he'll crack his knuckles,
Shake his beard,
Blink his eyes,
And let the breeze play in his hair.

He'll remember how different the sky used to look,
And how much closer it seems now.
There'd just be the one proud master of matter and architect of
    desires,
Between this Earth, and the Sun and the Moon.
He'll rumble, he'll nod, and he'll grant three wishes;
Only three,
Of whatever little mortal that holds the lamp
Between that blink of eternity.

In it's fingers, the Magick beyond the greatest magic:
That of human flesh, and of all desires that come along with it,
    and within it,
That put the ethereal being into its prison in the first place.

Yes, that day will come.
The Djinn will rise from his slumber,

And nations will look up in awe.

That day will come.

Three wishes will be granted, and the story of them coming
    true

Will be spoken of in songs and tales for centuries to come.

Even as the whispers die, the Djinn will be put to sleep again.

That day will come.

But for now, the sleeping Djinn dreams

Of open pastures, the pearly Moon,

The fluttering feeling of wind, and the silhouette of freedom
    outside the rusted lamp

That occasionally slips in along the walls,

When they decide to dust the antiques.

Today, the Djinn is going to sleep in late.

He has no one to answer wishes for.

He has no nations to overrule.

Nobody to goad into showing the deepest crevices of mortal
    desires.

Today, the lamp is forgotten.

The Moon is nowhere to be seen.

In his dreams though, there is always a full Moon, shining on
    ashen sands.

On Leaving

The branches of our cherry tree caught fire
The evening You promised to meet me in the rain.
The hemlock survived, but it doesn't feel familiar
Like it used to.
You'd know what I mean.
October's been a while, and the summers weren't kind.
Well, monsoons too,
But then that's monsoons for You.
Our glaciers shifted, melted,
Turned to water
And ran down gullies
Murmuring Your name.
Lightning struck our favourite rock,
And wildflower shrubs blossomed beautiful in the cracks,
A thousand nights ago.
They bloom violent and brave.
You'd have hated it.
I've left too, the last of my footsteps stopped echoing
In our place a few seasons ago.
I hated it too.
It got too loud
Once the gullies ran dry.

⟶◦◦◦⟵

آج کل (Aaj Kal)

Woh pyaar kal tha,
Par aaj kal nahi.
Main junoon nahi,
Tu sukoon nahi.

Tally

I remember falling in Love with you.
It gave me butterflies in my stomach,
And I fell in Love with the butterflies too.
It was only years after the last of them left
That I realised,
I'd forgotten how to fall out of Love.

Let's Not Call

We're fresh out of black and white in what feels like a 1940's
    film
In a theatre no one visits anymore.
Love,
Is rather not finding out than knowing
And knowing rather than dying.
Dying rather than being being hung out drying,
And drying rather than anything else that feels,
Like
Love…

Welling up in tears for an an ocean where
The last words of dying sailors fade
Clenching the photos of their loved ones that
No one remembers as much any more.

Love
Drains the colours out of your eyes and
Blinks the dreams out of your eyes, drawing sweat from your
    being,
As we remember the salt on our skin and the last gasps of us
    and we cry
Drowning past our last breath:

Our lungs full of us,
Our bones full of ashes
Our worlds full of oceans;
And we die over and over, forgotten past the shores of
Love.

There's only so far you can carry your swelling heart till
Your bones weigh heavier than your soul,
Carried in bodies that
Touch you with over and over until your soul
Breaks into a million pieces and your breath sets them on fire.

Love
Is the family madness personified
Running screaming into the nursery in the middle of the night
And laying their afterlife out to any presence
That'll take their soul in return for a slumber
In unending sunshine.
Shit,
Love,
Is the reason dogs howl into the night to make up for all the
    nights I couldn't stay up crying for you,
And mourning us than I mourn myself,
And know, if all the dogs in all the houses in all the alleys in all
    of the world
Cried with me, it'd still not be lou enough.

Sleep. Hold me. Cuddle in close. Please.

Whisper fairy tales to me, honey,

Damn the burning roofs and walls.

Whisper into my ears the stories of forever,

Of everything that you didn't touch that could have been a
    happy ending.

Love,

Is your friends picking up the breadcrumbs trails of

I told you so!

When your words starve my ears ringing with the echoes of
    you telling me…

"We'll leave this earth barren and open to the vultures, and
    hope someday

Through the cracks

The welling of a thousand years worth of tears

Finally makes it worth this lifetime."

Love,

Is the end to all ends,

The fever to all malaise,

The paracetamol to living,

And the last thing we remember before we aren't us.

I love you, and I don't know what to do with all the love

In my bones,

In my body,

In my being,

In this fever that doesn't shake off my bones,

Is what I'll tell you looking into your eyes.

Love, you were

The reason I can't wait to tell you everything you need to hear,

If only I could stay the night.

دھواں (Dhuwaan)

Kaum se bewafa

Wajah se nalayak

Sirat se berukhe

Rooh ye bafalak

Madhoshi ke raaho me

Khanah badoshi ki baaho me

Khoye huwe hai maatam me

Itne ke udaasi reh gaya,

Aur wajah udaasi ki bhool gaye

Hazaar saalo ki baarish ke dhund me.

Taras taras gaye, barso beete.

Garaj baraste tezaab se jaise

Sapne hi the,

Sehra me base iss zindagi me

Ishq me aapke waar ke wajah hum

Jeete jeete marte hi gaye.

Kagaar kagaar me maut ke aaghosh me,

Boond boond jo kashish lahoo me aaye

Jaan hamare puchhte reh gaye

"Aaye ho aaj, aap ho ya aab?"

Pighal ke bikhar ke raakh hote aaye iss tezaab ke

Dhuwan me,
Aur poochhte hi reh gaye,
"Aaye ho aaj,
Khwaab ho ya azaab?"

Johnny Appleseed's Last

To the backdrop of 3:37 Blues,
My neighbour disappeared from the place
I've been making houses in,
On nights like these.
I'd mourn, but instead,
Tonight, I drink
Because I don't want to feel what it's like
To build houses in this place,
And fill them all with you.

Sundowner Blues

I walked across my city and I walked into the cemetery,
Only to realise
Twenty minutes, thirteen seconds, and four cigarettes later,
That there was the kind of Love all around me in that place,
That You'd forgotten to pack when you left.
It was sad, man, it was just
So quiet.

You would have hated it.

Years had crumbled, wasted
So many of the stones, and yet I read
Leaning forward, squinting:
Poetry, declarations of love.
Odes to memories on every stone that still had a face.
It was hard to see, but it was there,
When the Sun peeked out from behind those grey clouds.
It had started to rain, and my heart was on fire.

D'you wanna know… No, no, I'll tell you,

I'll tell you how I got these scars.

See, all those beautiful butterflies, that are supposed to be live
somewhere else now

Came flocking out of my mouth and eyes.

All the way from where I first felt them.

I guess the ones that were left behind finally found the door I
couldn't.

And they flew.

They left, and I felt those butterflies as they rushed past my
heart,

Some of their wings still singed and crisp on their way out.

I lit my fifth from their wings.

I guarded my burning cigarette under my palm, near my sleeve,

Where I wear my heart.

Do You want to know how I got these scars?

I light my cigarettes too close to my face

And let them burn till my lips speak and

Speak poetry and stories

Till they can't.

And then I speak, because I'm an idiot.

I move my lips and they bleed poetry.

It tastes like Home.

I wanted to feel homeless in my city, because I wanted to really
feel

What it's like to not belong to the place you knew for sure
Was Home.
And as I waited there in the rain, to feel,
I remembered reading somewhere…

(Don't ask me where because my memory is a dilapidated building that's a safety hazard for its residents and it doesn't even have a sign and sometimes in the nights the pipes leak and you can feel things moving wait what was this story I can't remember but I DID read…)

"Home is where you go when you want to forget the world's on
    fire."

I called us Home.

I found my favourite piece of plank and some paint,
And hung it above the door, for all good homes have a sign up
    front;
And on it, I wrote the word:
"Universe".
I know. I wrote something sappy on a piece of dead wood. Fine!
It's washed off now in the rain.
And here I am, out in the world.
Feeling homeless for kicks.

It's raining.

And there's butterflies on fire.

⋘◦◦◦⋙

Troll Witch 2

Upon my ribs, she croons.

"There are days that I could eat your heart out.

Then again, there are days like these,

When I should really eat you whole, were I not worried about
　　what your

Insides would do

To my insides.

Tell me,"

She breathes down my neck,

"What'd you have go last?"

I think of the summer, where I learnt how you make wine taste.

How your breath feels.

How you move, and let my fingers trace maps that go places.

Here, and here, and here.

I think of what you'd look like right now, and years after,

At the end of the world, after all the seasons,

Past Apocalypse Avenue,

In the place we made Home.

I whisper,

"Bones, once it's winter."

كل خير سيعود لكع كل خير سيعود لكع كل خير سيعود لكع

About the Author

Sohom Paul is not sure what he is but a storyteller, and everything is a story to him. Should he get therapy? Should he channel his work into art?

Should he put a teaser for his next book in here?

He is a mysterious man, and no one knows. He doesn't, so believes no one does.

What does one, so convinced of stories, do when presented with the unfolding narrative of the universe?

Do they listen? Do they speak?

Sohom falls. And floats.

www.ingramcontent.com/pod-product-compliance
Lightning Source LLC
Chambersburg PA
CBHW021207130726
47988CB00002B/540